A Rachel Rosary

A RACHEL ROSARY

Intercessory Prayer
for Victims of
Post-Abortion Syndrome
Rev. Larry Kupferman

Resurrection Press
An Imprint of
CATHOLIC BOOK PUBLISHING CO.
Totowa • New Jersey

Nihil Obstat: Rev. Francis J. Schneider, J.C.D.
Censor librorum
January 24, 1994

Imprimatur: Most Rev. John R. McGann, D.D.
Bishop of Rockville Centre
March 3, 1994

The Nihil obstat and the imprimatur are declarations that work is considered to be free from doctrinal or moral error. It is not implied that those who have granted the same agree with the contents, opinions or statements expressed.

First published in 1994 by Resurrection Press, Ltd.
P.O. Box 248, Williston Park, NY 11596

Copyright © Larry Kupferman

ISBN: 1-878718-21-5

Cover design: John Murello

Butterfly on cover and pages 13, 16, 20, 23, 29, 33 and 37 of text, "SM" National Office of Post-Abortion Reconciliation and Healing

Printed in the United States of America.

6 7 8 9 10

Dedication

To Bernie and Dolly Saperstein, my grandparents, who, in raising me and their other eight grandchildren taught me how truly precious all life is, and how powerful forgiving love can be.

Acknowledgments

This began as a personal prayer experience which I shared with a friend. I am grateful to that friend, Fr. Tom McCormick, for pushing me to complete the project. I am also grateful to Fr. John Dillon, who read the first draft and encouraged me to contact the publisher. I would also like to thank my editor, Dr. Nancy Benvenga, for her guidance and suggestions. The New Life Prayer Community and the St. Kilian Right to Life Committee were the "guinea pigs" who first prayed the Rachel Rosary and found it an experience worthy of sharing with others. To these brothers and sisters I am truly grateful. And finally, for anything that I accomplish I give thanks to my Lord and Savior Jesus Christ. To him be all glory!

Foreword

I REMEMBER his voice. Concerned, pained, yet confident and strong. The voice of a healer. The sound of a person of prayer.

I remember his words. "John, there are more and more women and men coming to me confessing a past experience of abortion. Their suffering runs so deep. How can I help?" His words spoke with compassion, sensitivity and mercy.

I remember his eyes. We met not long after we initially spoke. His eyes were filled with life and hope. The light within was fired by the love he has for Christ and our Blessed Mother. They were the eyes of a faithful man seeking to be an instrument of God's healing grace to a broken world.

I remember his conviction. A drive, a resolve, a commitment that has energized his special ministry to the unborn and to those grieving the loss of an aborted child. A Spirit of Life compelling him to defend and foster life in all its stages and forms.

The voice, words, eyes and conviction I speak of come from one person: Fr. Larry Kupferman. The text that you are about to read is an expression of a soul-filled man whose life has been a source of strength and hope for so many. Do not simply read these words and reflections — pray them. Let the beautiful and powerful prayer tradition of the rosary widen your heart, deepen your spirit and touch your soul.

Thank you, Larry, for a wonderful gift.

Rev. John J. Dillon
February 1994

Introduction

IN JUNE 1990 I attended a conference with hundreds of priests and deacons at the Franciscan University of Steubenville in Ohio. During the week we were all at a Eucharistic Holy Hour in the main chapel where I was moved by an experience of prayer that would profoundly affect my priestly ministry. As I prayed before the Lord in the Blessed Sacrament, my meditation led me to contemplate the sanctity of a child in the womb. In my prayer, the identification of a child with the Lord himself was so powerful that I believed that this was something I should continue to pray about.

After Benediction I went outside to where there is a tomb with a perpetual flame in honor of the victims of abortion. I prayed by the tomb and was convinced in my prayer that the Lord desired me to use my priestly ministry to become more active in the Right-to-Life cause.

I went home from that conference and continued to pray for direction as to how the Lord wanted me to serve him in this area. I have never felt that it was my call to picket in front of abortion clinics or become a political activist. But I knew that something more than my occasional preaching in defense of the sacredness of life was necessary. The answer soon came.

The week following that conference, three different people came to me in my office, confessing (either sacramentally or in the context of seeking counseling) one or more abortions in which they had taken part.

The first of these was a married man who was upset over a decision that he and his wife had made some years earlier. Their doctor had advised them to terminate a pregnancy because of the probability that the child would be born severely handicapped. Now, as they were trying again to conceive, he was overwhelmed with guilt and a feeling that they no longer "deserved" to have a baby.

The second was a teenage girl who had recently aborted because she was afraid of facing her parents as well as her peers. Her close friends tried to persuade her to have the baby but she was too afraid, and now she was afraid that God could never forgive her.

The third was a young adult woman who came to see me at the advice of her friend because she was having such a terrible time with her self-esteem. During the course of our conversation she revealed that she had had two abortions and felt "like a hypocrite" going to church or even having friends who were involved in her parish.

Each of these three persons was suffering from what I was later to learn was Post-Abortion Syndrome, the term for the unresolved guilt, grief, regret and loss associated with those who have had a previous experience of abortion. Here was the answer to my prayer.

I called Fr. John Dillon, a friend who had started Project Rachel in my diocese. Project Rachel is a ministry of healing for victims of Post-Abortion Syndrome. It takes its name from Jeremiah 31:15-17:

> In Ramah is heard the sound of moaning,
> of bitter weeping! Rachel mourns her children,
> she refuses to be consoled
> because her children are no more.
> Thus says the LORD:
> Cease your cries of mourning,
> wipe your eyes.
> The sorrow you have shown shall have its
> reward
> . . . .There is hope for your future.

I met with Fr. John and told him of my experience. Subsequently he trained me as a Project Rachel counselor. This is a wonderful ministry of healing directed toward those who suffer from Post-Abortion Syndrome.

Since that time I have been journeying with women from brokenness to wholeness in this process of healing so necessary for those who are the "other" victims of abortion. In this area of ministry I have witnessed the miracle of God's mercy before my very eyes. Women who came to me convinced that they were the most unlovable dredges of the earth have moved to the point of accepting God's forgiveness for their sins; they have traveled through the process of grieving over their lost children and are able to praise God with genuine smiles on their faces! What a gift God has given me to participate in this conferral of his grace.

Perhaps the greatest lesson that the Holy Spirit has taught me in this process is to see how important it is that those of us who profess to be "pro-life" lend compassionate and loving support to those who have been duped into choosing abortion, for whatever reason.

This past year I returned to that tomb in Steubenville to pray for the Post-Abortion Syndrome victims with whom I have been working. This time, as I felt moved to pray a rosary on their behalf, I asked the Lord to help me to put these people's concerns in the forefront of my prayer. As I meditated on the Sorrowful Mysteries, I was reminded of various experiences that these people shared with me. It was then that the idea of the Rachel Rosary was born.

As a priest I have been privileged to share in the stories of those who are broken and in search of God's healing. In that capacity I have witnessed first-hand the effects of Post-Abortion Syndrome and the feelings of alienation that accompany it. The meditations that follow are gleaned from experiences shared with me by women who have come to me through Project Rachel. They are the real-life burdens that these women and many other persons must so often bear in silence. When I pray these meditations, they help me to be more in solidarity with those who suffer from Post-Abortion Syndrome. I hope the same can happen for you.

The Rachel Rosary can be prayed privately, with a prayer group, or as a paraliturgical prayer event in the parish. In a group setting I suggest using two speakers: a "Lector" to read the Scripture passages that introduce each mystery, and a "Prayer Leader" to announce each intention and begin the "Hail Mary."

A Rachel Rosary

The Creed

THIS STATEMENT of faith speaks of the divine origin of all life, and of the hope promised to all who rely on the statements proclaimed within it. We recite the Creed in order to affirm our identity as members of God's family, the Church. Our oneness expressed in our faith connects us to one another, to God and to all God's sons and daughters, living and dead.

I believe in God the Father almighty, Creator of heaven and earth, and in Jesus Christ, his only Son, our Lord, who was conceived by the Holy Spirit, born of the Virgin Mary, suffered under Pontius Pilate, was crucified, died and was buried. He descended into hell; on the third day he arose again from the dead. He ascended into heaven and sits at the right hand of the Father; from thence he shall come to judge the living and the dead.

I believe in the Holy Spirit, the holy Catholic Church, the communion of saints, the forgiveness of sins, the resurrection of the body and life everlasting. Amen.

Our Father

We acknowledge the fatherhood of God and offer this rosary for God's children who suffer from Post-Abortion Syndrome.

Our Father who art in heaven, hallowed be thy name. Thy kingdom come. Thy will be done on earth as it is in heaven.

Give us this day our daily bread, and forgive us our trespasses as we forgive those who trespass against us; and lead us not into temptation, but deliver us from evil. Amen.

Hail Mary for Faith

We pray for an increase of faith for these children of God, so that they may come to believe in the mercy of God.

Hail Mary full of grace, the Lord is with thee. Blessed art thou among women and blessed is the fruit of thy womb, Jesus.

Holy Mary, mother of God, pray for us sinners, now and at the hour of our death. Amen.

Hail Mary for Hope

We pray for an increase of hope for these children of God, so that they can look forward to the joy of redeemed lives.

Hail Mary. . .

Hail Mary for Love

We pray for an increase of love for these children of God, that they will be able to accept the love of God and know true love in their hearts.

Hail Mary. . .

Glory be to the Father, and to the Son, and to the Holy Spirit, as it was in the beginning, is now and ever shall be, world without end. Amen.

The Agony in the Garden

THEN THEY CAME to a place named Gethsemane, and he said to his disciples, "Sit here while I pray." He took with him Peter, James, and John, and began to be troubled and distressed. Then he said to them, "My soul is sorrowful even to death. Remain here and keep watch." He advanced a little and fell to the ground and prayed that if it were possible the hour might pass him by; he said, "Abba, Father, all things are possible to you. Take this cup away from me, but not what I will but what you will." When he returned he found them asleep. He said to Peter, "Simon, are you asleep? Could you not keep watch for one hour? Watch and pray that you may not undergo the test. The spirit is willing but the flesh is weak." Withdrawing again, he prayed, saying the same thing. Then he returned once more and found them asleep, for they could not keep their eyes open and did not know what to answer him. He returned a third time and said to them, "Are you still sleeping and taking your rest? It is enough. The hour has come. Behold the Son of Man is to be handed over to sinners. Get up, let us go. See, my betrayer is at hand. (Mark 14:32-42)

We pray this decade, keeping in mind the agony that accompanies a decision to abort.

Our Father. . .

Ten Hail Marys

1. For the thirteen-year-old girl who is pregnant and afraid.

   Hail Mary. . .

2. For the teenager who is pregnant and afraid to tell her parents.

   Hail Mary. . .

3. For the young woman whose boyfriend abandons her when the pregnancy is discovered.

   Hail Mary. . .

4. For the young woman who, alone and afraid, gets "counseled" at the abortion clinic.

   Hail Mary. . .

5. For the woman who got pregnant to save a relationship, only to find that her lover has run away at the news.

   Hail Mary. . .

6. For the mother of a poor family who unexpectedly becomes pregnant and is advised that abortion is the "logical" choice for her family's sake.

   Hail Mary. . .

7. For the couple who is pregnant with a child suspected of having a birth defect.

   Hail Mary. . .

8. For the man who fathers a child he wasn't expecting and who believes that abortion will free him.

   Hail Mary. . .

9. For the doctor who advises a couple to abort their child and thinks he is helping.

Hail Mary. . .

10. For the school counselor who believes that advising a student to abort her baby is saving her future.

Hail Mary. . .

Glory be to the Father, and to the Son, and to the Holy Spirit, as it was in the beginning, is now and ever shall be, world without end. Amen.

The Scourging at the Pillar

SO PILATE, wishing to satisfy the crowd, released
Barabbas to them and, after he had Jesus scourged,
handed him over to be crucified. (Mark 15:15)

We pray this decade, keeping in mind the pain, both
emotional and physical, that accompanies a decision to
participate in the killing of one's own child.

Our Father. . .

Ten Hail Marys

1. For the teenager who suffers the pain of sitting in fear
   in the clinic waiting room.

   Hail Mary. . .

2. For the girl who suffers the pain of forced labor to kill
   her child.

   Hail Mary. . .

3. For the husband and wife whose sexual intimacy is negatively affected by the scars of an abortion.

   Hail Mary...

4. For the pain felt by a victim of Post-Abortion Syndrome each time he or she beholds a new-born child.

   Hail Mary...

5. For the woman whose pain and guilt over a previous abortion manifests as clinical depression years later.

   Hail Mary...

6. For the woman who bears the pain of feeling a life literally being sucked out of her.

   Hail Mary...

7. For the woman whose body is so damaged that she can never again bear a child.

   Hail Mary...

8. For the man who suffers the pain of knowing that his child was aborted against his will.

   Hail Mary. . .

9. For the physician who actively takes a life under the guise of medical "care."

   Hail Mary. . .

10. For the counselor who bears the pain of knowing that a child is dead due to his counsel.

    Hail Mary. . .

    Glory be to the Father, and to the Son, and to the Holy Spirit, as it was in the beginning, is now and ever shall be, world without end. Amen.

The Crowning with Thorns

THE SOLDIERS led him away inside the palace, that is, the praetorium and assembled the whole cohort. They clothed him in purple and weaving a crown of thorns, placed it on him. They began to salute him with, "Hail, King of the Jews!" and kept striking his head with a reed and spitting upon him. They knelt before him in homage. And when they had mocked him, they stripped him of the purple cloak, dressed him in his own clothes, and led him out to crucify him.
(Mark 15:16-20)

We pray this decade, keeping in mind the humiliation that a person who has an abortion must endure, if not initially, then inevitably.

Our Father. . .

Ten Hail Marys

1. For the fourteen-year-old girl who cannot face her own mother.

   Hail Mary...

2. For the woman who cannot read articles related to abortion without feeling great humiliation.

   Hail Mary...

3. For the teenage girl who stays active in her youth group at church, fearfully hiding the truth during their devotions and discussions.

   Hail Mary...

4. For the teenager who becomes pregnant after boasting about how "careful" she and her boyfriend are.

   Hail Mary...

5. For the man or woman who is a parish minister and who cries inside when the issue of abortion is raised.

   Hail Mary...

6. For the woman who has had to see her daughter

become a young woman but does not feel equipped to speak about sex.

Hail Mary. . .

7. For the woman whose humiliation at being pregnant forces her to act against her values.

   Hail Mary. . .

8. For the man who knows the humiliation of having decided to end the life of his own first-born son or daughter.

   Hail Mary. . .

9. For the physician who teaches interns to deliver babies while he himself is killing them.

   Hail Mary. . .

10. For the counselor who allows the pressure of "political correctness" to influence her counsel.

    Hail Mary. . .

    Glory be to the Father, and to the Son, and to the Holy Spirit, as it was in the beginning, is now and ever shall be, world without end. Amen.

The Carrying of the Cross

SO THEY TOOK JESUS, and carrying the cross himself he went out to what is called the Place of the Skull, in Hebrew, Golgotha. (John 19:17)

We pray this decade, keeping in mind the guilt that burdens those who are victims of abortion.

Our Father. . .

Ten Hail Marys

1. For the girl who cannot look her parents in the eye because of what she has done.

   Hail Mary. . .

2. For the teenager who contemplates suicide, convinced that she no longer deserves to live.

   Hail Mary. . .

3. For the young woman who cannot enter a church because she feels so unclean.

   Hail Mary. . .

4. For the couple who believe they will not be able to conceive another child as a punishment for their "crime."

   Hail Mary. . .

5. For the woman whose guilt keeps her from allowing anyone to love her.

   Hail Mary. . .

6. For the woman whose guilt will not allow her to discipline her own children.

   Hail Mary. . .

7. For the woman or man who, filled with guilt, cannot accept even the sacramental forgiveness of God.

   Hail Mary. . .

8. For the man who insists that his wife have an abortion and feels no responsibility himself.

Hail Mary. . .

9. For the physician who kills babies on a daily basis, yet feels no remorse.

Hail Mary. . .

10. For the counselor who encourages abortion as a means of birth control.

Hail Mary. . .

Glory be to the Father, and to the Son, and to the Holy Spirit, as it was in the beginning, is now and ever shall be, world without end. Amen.

The Crucifixion

AT NOON darkness came over the whole land until three in the afternoon. And at three o'clock Jesus cried out in a loud voice, *"Eloi, Eloi, lema sabachthani?"* which is translated, "My God, my God, why have you forsaken me?" Some of the bystanders who heard it said, "Look, he is calling Elijah." One of them ran, soaked a sponge with wine, put it on a reed, and gave it to him to drink, saying, "Wait, let us see if Elijah comes to take him down." Jesus gave a loud cry and breathed his last. The veil of the sanctuary was torn in two from top to bottom. When the centurion who stood facing him saw how he breathed his last he said, "Truly this man was the Son of God!" There were also women looking on from a distance. Among them were Mary Magdalene, Mary the mother of the younger James and of Joses, and Salome. These women had followed him when he was in Galilee and ministered to him. There were also many other women who had come up with him to Jerusalem. (Mark 15:33-41)

We pray this decade, keeping in mind the many types of death that accompany abortion; but at the same time we hold fast to the hope that is always offered by God and is so desperately needed by those who suffer the pain of Post-Abortion Syndrome.

Our Father. . .

Ten Hail Marys

1. For the child who dies in the womb of his or her mother.

   Hail Mary. . .

2. For the young mother who dies as a result of an abortion procedure.

   Hail Mary. . .

3. For the spiritual death of a woman who undergoes an abortion procedure.

   Hail Mary. . .

4. For the death of a relationship between a young woman and her lover as a result of an abortion experience.

   Hail Mary...

5. For the marriage that dies as a result of an abortion.

   Hail Mary...

6. For the death of the dreams of a young girl who is stifled by her feelings of guilt.

   Hail Mary...

7. For the many small deaths that occur over and over again in the life of the woman or man who cannot accept the healing forgiveness of God.

   Hail Mary...

8. For the emotional death of a man who would abandon his lover and his child as a matter of convenience.

   Hail Mary...

9. For the physician who uses his life-giving training to terminate the lives of children in the womb.

Hail Mary. . .

10. For the moral death of the clinic counselor who spends his days counseling women to kill their babies.

Hail Mary. . .

Glory be to the Father, and to the Son, and to the Holy Spirit, as it was in the beginning, is now and ever shall be, world without end. Amen.

The Glorious Mystery of the Resurrection

BUT MARY stayed outside the tomb weeping. And as she wept, she bent over into the tomb and saw two angels in white sitting there, one at the head and one at the feet where the body of Jesus had been. And they said to her, "Woman, why are you weeping?" She said to them, "They have taken my Lord, and I don't know where they laid him." When she had said this, she turned around and saw Jesus there, but did not know it was Jesus. Jesus said to her, "Woman, why are you weeping? Whom are you looking for?" She thought it was the gardener and said to him, "Sir, if you carried him away, tell me where you laid him, and I will take him." Jesus said to her, "Mary!" She turned and said to him in Hebrew, "Rabbouni," which means Teacher. Jesus said to her, "Stop holding on to me, for I have not yet ascended to the Father. But go to my brothers and tell them, 'I am going to my Father and your Father, to my God and your God!' " Mary of Magdala went and announced to the disciples, "I have seen the Lord," and what he told her. (John 20:11-18)

We pray this decade, keeping in mind the faith in a renewed and strengthened life that is offered to all who suffer from Post-Abortion Syndrome.

Our Father. . .

Ten Hail Marys

1. For an increase in love and communication between parents and their children.

Hail Mary. . .

2. For an increase in education in the areas of sexuality and relationships.

Hail Mary. . .

3. For an increase in the number of compassionate pro-life leaders.

Hail Mary. . .

4. For increased sensitivity towards those who have been victimized by abortion.

Hail Mary. . .

5. For courage on the part of those who suffer from Post-Abortion Syndrome, that they might step forward and welcome the healing process into their lives.

   Hail Mary. . .

6. For an increase in pregnancy services that offer realistic alternatives to abortion.

   Hail Mary. . .

7. In thanksgiving for the many counselors who accompany victims of Post-Abortion Syndrome on their journey toward healing.

   Hail Mary. . .

8. In thanksgiving for the men who support their partners in bringing the joy of unexpected new life into the world.

   Hail Mary. . .

9. In thanksgiving for the doctors who reverence life in all its stages and propose constructive solutions to an unexpected pregnancy.

Hail Mary. . .

10. In thanksgiving for the counselors who recognize the need to teach responsibility with our God-given sexuality.

Hail Mary. . .

Glory be to the Father, and to the Son, and to the Holy Spirit, as it was in the beginning, is now and ever shall be, world without end. Amen.

WE CONCLUDE OUR PRAYER for those who have been victimized by abortion by invoking the intercession of Mary, who in her own acceptance of the "sword that pierced her heart" can identify with all parents who grieve. Let us pray the "Hail, Holy Queen."

Hail, holy Queen, mother of mercy, our life, our sweetness and our hope. To thee do we cry, poor banished children of Eve. To thee do we send up our sighs, mourning and weeping in this vale of tears. Turn then, most gracious advocate, thine eyes of mercy toward us, and after this our exile show unto us the blessed fruit of thy womb, Jesus. O clement, O loving, O sweet Virgin Mary.

V. *Pray for us, O holy mother of God*
R. *That we may be made worthy of the promises of Christ.*

We believe that those who have been prayed for in this rosary will be touched by God's Spirit and that hearts will be changed. Where there is brokenness there can be healing. Where there are hearts of stone, there can be hearts of flesh (Ezekiel 36:26). We who respect and support the sacredness of all life must continue to pray for all of God's children. Let us do so with faith, with hope and with compassion!

A PATH TO HOPE
for Parents of Aborted Children and Those Who Minister to Them

JOHN J. DILLON

Drawing on his considerable experience with parents of aborted children, Fr. Dillon describes the spiritual and psychological aftermath of abortion and offers solid guidelines and compassionate advice to those who counsel, minister to or journey with them.

"One of the most valuable resources available on the complexities of abortion."—FR. GERALD TWOMEY

"Fr. Dillon proves himself a gifted and experienced counselor in this field."—*The Priest*

80pp. $5.95

Also available in audiocassette, 60 min., $6.95

Resurrection Press
P.O. Box 248, Williston Park, NY 11596
1-800-89 BOOKS

Additional Titles Published by Resurrection Press, a Catholic Book Publishing Imprint

A Rachel Rosary Larry Kupferman	$4.50
Blessings All Around Dolores Leckey	$8.95
Catholic Is Wonderful Mitch Finley	$4.95
Come, Celebrate Jesus! Francis X. Gaeta	$4.95
From Holy Hour to Happy Hour Francis X. Gaeta	$7.95
Healing through the Mass Robert DeGrandis, SSJ	$9.95
Our Grounds for Hope Fulton J. Sheen	$7.95
The Healing Rosary Mike D.	$5.95
Healing Your Grief Ruthann Williams, OP	$7.95
Heart Peace Adolfo Quezada	$9.95
Life, Love and Laughter Jim Vlaun	$7.95
Living Each Day by the Power of Faith Barbara Ryan	$8.95
The Joy of Being a Catechist Gloria Durka	$4.95
The Joy of Being a Eucharistic Minister Mitch Finley	$5.95
The Joy of Being a Lector Mitch Finley	$5.95
The Joy of Being an Usher Gretchen Hailer, RSHM	$5.95
Lights in the Darkness Ave Clark, O.P.	$8.95
Loving Yourself for God's Sake Adolfo Quezada	$5.95
Personally Speaking Jim Lisante	$8.95
Practicing the Prayer of Presence van Kaam/Muto	$8.95
5-Minute Miracles Linda Schubert	$4.95
Season of New Beginnings Mitch Finley	$4.95
Season of Promises Mitch Finley	$4.95
Soup Pot Ethel Pochocki	$8.95
Stay with Us John Mullin, SJ	$3.95
Surprising Mary Mitch Finley	$7.95
Teaching as Eucharist Joanmarie Smith	$5.95
What He Did for Love Francis X. Gaeta	$5.95
You Are My Beloved Mitch Finley	$10.95
Your Sacred Story Robert Lauder	$6.95